AF244113

Other works by Peter Frickel

Kaleen

River

Lilies of the Vlei:
My Life in Amanzimtoti, South Africa

Lotha and the Three Crosses

Roads

To learn more about the author,
his life and his writings,
please visit his website:
www.peterfrickel.com.

My Frog Sings

My Frog Sings

Peter Frickel

ISBN-13: 978-0985190002
ISBN-10: 0985190000

Issued as e-book under the title, *My Frog Sings: Thoughts and essays from the garden*, June 9, 2012.
First printing, 2018.

Published by Peter Frickel
Edited and designed by Melissa M. Manzanares
Printed by CreateSpace, An Amazon.com Company

Front cover credit:
Illustrations by Calia Frickel
Photographs by Peter Frickel

Contents

Something of Value

Everything that blooms, fades; everything that births, changes. Nothing stays the same. So, too, within the garden of my life, seasons come and go.

For a long time, I had thought of planting trees and shrubs and beds of flowers around our home. Instead, my life filled itself with career, security and providing family needs.

In my struggle to succeed, I stretched the pace of wealth building beyond good common sense. Exhausted, I found I was empty of myself.

Sidelined, parked with engine idling, I began to wonder: what next? For without direction, and not knowing what to do, helplessness becomes a haunting shadow.

Gradually as I searched, thoughts gathered and flowed into an idea, a start that eventually led to a beginning. Nothing sudden, just slow and casual... drips and drops into a pot that warmed. Additions brought the first steam.

I started a garden — a garden is life — but, surprisingly, it is a garden not built, but gathered piece by piece. First one weed less. Then, something planted to show a difference.

Like friendship, there is a period of exploration, a choice made, effort to understand another world, talk and chatter on some things vague and not fully understood. A lot happens. There are great moments, many enduring, death always comes — nothing bears fruit all the time.

As I positioned pieces of my garden, opened soil with hoe and shovel, I learned to germinate seeds, plant and measure success by seasons. Time turned its pages, wrapped a new feeling around me and I became aware of the delicate moments that frame each success and disappointment.

Foliage grew tall, sometimes with patches of weeds that held big thorns, reminders of disappointments and past failures. I cleared them by hand, pulled them out by roots. In the same manner, I tried to rid myself of past ills.

All this time, I seemed to be investigating and unconsciously digging, looking to find fertile soil that might lie deep within. Now, I wanted to work this garden every day, make a success. For it had come without a past, brought freshness and freedom. It was clean and becoming a new part of me.

No more did I wish to ride rapids in my pirogue on the Congo River, gamble with its currents and sudden turns, spill over and lose everything. The current of life had drowned too many dreams. I was just trying to breathe, to hold a paddle, to guide my way out of turbulence to a quiet eddy to rest, to know I was alive, to try again.

Remarkably, the longer and harder I worked with a defined sense of responsibility—made purposeful decisions where to plant, what to transplant, what seeds to germinate and which trees to prune—the deeper I moved into the real purpose of my garden: to move away from turmoil and let old pain ease itself.

I became absorbed, focused and detached. Separated from the everyday world, I moved into the sound of peace whose rhythm began to beat and echo around me. Life widened, dreams of a new direction began to possess me; I was trying to love something again.

Now, Autumn had climbed through vines, weaved an invisible fabric of faded color, the shadow of a past glorious summer. While winter, unloved, had taken beauty, given death and buried itself in dried stems, frozen memories and scolded berries, it could not take away time.

Soon, the garden would feel my love, everything would come alive and a past of betrayal would fade into new beginnings. For now, I was with new friends... squirrels and raccoons, bees and butterflies, fat fresh worms, families of lizards and a toad called Gaudeamus Igitur who visited after the heavy rains.

Rebirth and the comfort of success came in seeds. Some thumped to the ground with the sound of overripe fruit; others floated on cusps of wind to escape and spread elsewhere like new ideas searching for a quiet corner. Then, there were those that ventured into distant places to germinate in solitude, to dream and grow into one self.

While I let some lie about the garden in the silence of friendship, undisturbed, I gathered others for germination, sorted sinkers from floaters as if plucking productive thoughts from idle dreams. Held in my hands, these new seeds felt like rain, pure and fresh, like a washing for a garden that loves to be soaked.

Oh! I should have learned this process as a child, but then it was different, and no one thought to teach me the way nature solves its problems.

When on my knees weeding flower beds or performing needed tasks that pull on stretched and tired limbs, I would smell richness in the earth and wonder how I might have blossomed in another soil. I wanted to watch little green shoots grow from planted seeds, watch God teaching in mysteries.

Creation had captured me. Secretly, each day, I wondered what seeds would I need to plant for my new life?

Gardening has many beginnings and endings—it is where the mind searches, where the body seeks origin, where both see tragedy written in color. Its growth is not held in some future idle expectation but alive in daily struggles, searching for synchronicity to guide it into time, to follow the Creator's path.

Unknowingly, when I started I thought it was only the results that counted. Time taught me that each growth was an individual effort, each plant different from the other, each needed its own understanding of care. Time taught me that there was a process of knowing and learning, that knowledge is not experience and to always ask how and what and never tempt why.

I must have been amongst friends for I felt hugged. Now I saw each person as an individual, separate in their own light, different from their shadow. I was beginning to think about my new world, hoping for sunshine.

It takes time and care to work your garden, to see new things. Not much grows without rain so I labored and toiled, gave it water and compost and life.

When heavy memories of the past revisit, I am pushed into loneliness. There, surrounded by the driest unloved soil of Africa—forgotten and unwanted, parched and cracked, stretched to the horizon—I am left by winds, to die.

I believe rain always comes and tears follow to wash away torments. They come because nothing lasts forever. When those first rains fall upon the dying plains, they draw that lovely sweet smell of petrichor and signal the start of new life.

They are the tears that roll down our cheeks, warm and salty. They come to wash away a lifeless look, leave a smile of new colors, and a shining light of hope within. Just as nature demands each season clear itself for another to enter, so too, I realized, only a buried past could open my gate.

I was trying to let the old river flow away, swim into the mouth of the new, where outflow meets tide, where I would feel the clean of the ocean.

Slowly, I had moved to start. I had begun to grow new choices and let a seedless past wither away. Usually, my early mornings were spent around the front driveway before heavy sun reached the elephant ears, a gathering place for my favorite lizard family.

Every year some of the family disappeared, perhaps to build a home elsewhere. Maybe "Old Brownie," the giant bull frog who lived in the crevice of a boulder, knew where. Certainly, Harry the blue jay, who grew heavier in the breeding season, showed no guilt; but through observance, I had my suspicions.

I loved to watch elephant ears sway close to the ground, heavy with sunning lizards wobbling on the surface while tiny newborn, no longer than a match stick, zipped across thick juicy stems.

Every morning they came and every morning I watched. We befriended one another as I fed them insects and gave each a name. Some were brave and ate from my hand. Some bobbed up and down and threw out full-colored throats that showed orange mouths with wobbling tongues.

Fabius Cunctator, the bravest, was the biggest and my favorite. We got to know each other, understood our presence and found friendship.

It does not matter how many people you know, how kind you are to them and how often you see them. Rather, it begs the question: how many friends do you have?

Fabius and I were friends throughout his long life, and all that time, he made me welcome in "our" garden. Hail Fabius!

Things do not last forever. His passing brought memories of strangers met, who showed kindness, shared joyous words, gave me true directions. Mostly, they laughed with me, for life could be hard on my traveled road.

I found a flat stone, a large one, and etched *Fabius* on its face, then placed it under the widest leaf for his family to recognize. I raised my shovel — the gardener's salute — wished him well, then swallowed a salty moistness resting in my mouth.

The feeling of raw wood — the hoe handle in my hands on a hot summer day — is a powerful tool. I work and leave little thought for anything else. The flow of sweat gathers across my forehead, the neck drips, the shoulder blades soak and I drink from large bottles of water. I carry Africa pushed into me. That capacity to burn in the sun, dig and plant and tend a garden loved in the midday heat; different from the dry desert heat and a slow walk with laden camels and Bedouin friends.

That was then, but this is home where summer days now beg me: dig and plant and care for visitors. There are vessels of water at the base of plants. The bird bath is full. Containers fixed between branches of the big oak are filled to overflow. Every day they come, from all directions, to drink and bathe and sing.

I remember names, welcome them, listen to songs of happiness and calls to mates, voices filled with strength, loud and energized. Soon they will start to build nests, lay eggs and raise little ones. There will be new families with new songs and only a short while to watch them share their love.

It will not last forever. They leave, gone till they return.

That gone holds emptiness. It brings silence. It takes away the lovely sound of song, of butterflies over lantana, magnolia blossoms, the smell of jasmine and little bud colors held at the end of delicate stems that creep along the ground.

Gone is like a family seemingly torn apart with empty days, black as old iron.

I stay and work. Differences show. I feel them. Once, I thought of the garden as soil and water, grass and trees and flowers, a life without feeling, only results. I have made new discoveries, penetrated, moved into a world of recognition, added smells, sounds, and cries from feathered and furry friends... and intoxicating thoughts.

Tired after a full day's work, I seek the oak that shades; gather cool water from a rain barrel, mix it with wild honey made by guests wandering through.

Stretched flat on the ground, I look up through layers of leaf-laden limbs into the sky; sweet water comforts, eases away tiredness.

Relaxed, I drift with the breeze to watch an eagle riding wind currents. A Martial Eagle, master of wind and distant runs, gliding across open sky. Eyesight unparalleled, he can see me, even smell me from that distance. I cannot hide, I cannot run. I must know all my problems before I can find the true answer.

In this late summer afternoon, clouds gather, bind, argue, twist and turn in anger; the earth prays for rain. Thunder crashes, lightning streaks and voices wake me from a dream:

"Where are you... where are you?

Hurry, it's going to rain—there's lightning."

To Love is to Serve

In this little world, surrounded by time, growth and the mystery of my garden, it is good to feel that there is a cure for all ills. No one is unwanted, unloved, or forgotten. This garden comforts emotions and accommodates the hurt that lies deep within. Nothing is demanded. There are no questions, just giving and acceptance, humility and a search for truth that requires patience.

Here, I have become a giver, a nurturer, and a provider of nourishment. I am the keeper of this little space with its trees and fruit and bird nests. It is a home for little furry friends, for beds of enriched soil where vines creep into corners, where their buds seek sun, grow, blossom, and blow scent.

It is the Creator's garden where He holds dominion. There is no whisperer, no musician, only secrets.

The earth is calm. Its womb holds planted seeds set in measured lines, silent in beds of soil and compost. As I think of each seed—its upheaval, its struggle and its quiet desperation to travel toward sunlight—I feel I am remembering me.

Some plants grow freely. For others the journey of life and its expectations exact all strength. Their stems languish. Drained, they clutch petals that show the look of soon to go. There is no cosmetician, no immediate cure, just memories of a fearful resting place—the compost heap for the failed—and I feel the heat of my determination.

I work soil with sun and rain, choose seeds, measure their compost and plan their shade. I guide their struggle to reach the light, knowing there are moments in each life when nothing can replace care, a gentle word, a tender touch and a soft voice that strokes emotions.

To gather a garden is a promise to protect and provide and build a compost heap. Save little pieces about the garden and home. Added, they enrich.

In the early morning, with squirrels running branches, a blue jay in the bird bath, and a promised hot clear day, I began to assemble materials.

There's a plan, a direction and an opportunity, that could lead to innovation and creation. My obligation to build is a chance to try something new. It is also a promise of completion.

I begin.

The stakes to hold chicken wire were metal. As I pounded them into the ground, the sound rang and echoed. I heard it. Again, then again and in a childhood reflection, its ringing plunged me into the Valley of a Thousand Hills, to roam and rebound, swoop deep, stretch further, then disappear into the far hills, gone forever.

Some beautiful sounds and feelings do not stay for long. I do not know where they hide or when they might return. They just happen. When they pass, I feel cleansed, touched by soft silk, and compassionate toward my surroundings.

The compost heap was oblong. It lay in partial shade, open to sun at the edge of the oak's long branches. It welcomed rain and dried in sunshine. This allowed it to act and react in chemical fashion, as long as I followed the rule of one green layer covered by one brown layer.

Freshly mowed grass was covered by a layer of moist brown leaves while fresh pruned oak leaves were covered by raked debris from the garden. Between these sandwiched layers went coffee-grinds and vegetable peelings from the kitchen.

Layer after layer lay buried like stretched memories from each season, never to be recaptured.

Covered by time, they mix and crumble. Turned by rake and fork, they get to know each other. Slowly, the chameleon of time and science change them into another entity, a powerful comfort and the lifeblood of my garden. I was beginning to see how changes bring new opportunities.

This rich brown compost is set around roots and sprinkled over newly planted seeds. As I spread, I become aware of how long it takes to change some things, how necessary understanding and patience are, how a powerful new form can help.

Seeded areas need regular visits so with buckets of compost and sharpened tools I prune, hoe, weed and feed, check for bad bugs and diseases.

The work is gentle. It satisfies curiosity. It is also thrilling when I find and feel little shoots, fresh from their struggle through the earth. I welcome them and promise care. They are the strength of a new life; they are me in search.

Different seasons come, each brings change. Sometimes it's the fruit trees that bend with bounty and smell of ripening. Sometimes it's the plants with little buds that burst, flower, throw color and float perfume. Sometimes it is the move of oaks skyward, wearing green.

In the cold, the garden shows a silent face. It is without smile, colorless. It suffers in the silence of winter. The sun does not stretch through to warm each ridge of the Carambola and without its spread across the surface of the ground, sweet potatoes brown their leaves, stay rooted deep in the shadow of the earth, feeling forward in darkness, every day, waiting for change. I wonder... will anything ever grow here again?

Nothing stays the same; everything changes with time. Once I walked between sand dunes and wadis seeing only mirage after mirage dancing over desert sands. Now, I begin to see a horizon spotted with opportunities and feel an early glow of passion to create.

We must move toward change.

We must move from our broken selves, from our bare foreign soil or a place once called home, to find a home within.

We must seek a special place to germinate, for we have a need to love, a need to fulfill ourselves and our dreams.

Some plants, like people, cripple their start. Their seeds never move from the shade. They choose their own winter, suck their sap and fade. Sometimes I see that shadow pass close by.

The mysteries in my garden lie dormant. Unchanged bulbs and seeds and tubers sleep in secret with patience. They are the ones that never give up. They try season after season. Then suddenly, with an indefatigable spirit, they break through. They bud and blossom and my world fills with color. I wonder how it happens.

These are the late bloomers that live in my garden and stand sprinkled amongst friends. Whenever they surface, I watch and wonder and try to understand their secret. They are a special seed. Their purpose strengthens me, and I realize I have other pathways about my garden to explore.

Fruit Ripens and I am Sweetened

My garden is a space. It is time with a beginning and an end, between which nothing stays the same. It is a place where so much comes and goes and nothing lasts forever. It is where nature measures seasons—where I measure my life.

As I walked towards the hills on a rutted road of soil and rock, I heard them singing. They tilled and planted. For generations, their hoes in unison have turned this earth. Some worked with babies strapped to their backs, the old with drooping breasts, the young and the children with playful smiles. There are no men.

They sang as they toiled, sowed seed as they worked, sang continuously for a harvest and the joy of fertility.

Under this fierce African sun, there is no shade, only a dark fear that nature will turn its back on their digging and hoeing and planting.

Last year the rains came, brought abundance, harvests for everyone and more corn to brew beer. It had not been this good for several years.

"We hope for another good harvest, so we can eat well, and I can have another baby." She laughed out loudly.

"Every year is different, and when everything grows, the cows give plenty of milk. Other years, we grow thin. The old do not survive. Hungry lions roam the village. We cannot always say what will happen."

The duty of the gardener is driven by discipline while luck is God's choice.

Each season I measure the results of my efforts, each garden group separately. Those findings are never compared with the results and ideals and achievements of others. We are each our own garden.

When nature moves its boundaries—those between seasons, with different strengths of sunshine and varying inches of rainfall—I see experience smile. My results are from skills gathered over time, from endeavors joyous and pleasurable, backbreaking and disappointing, dreamt of on the fields of hope and passion.

The final judgment of my personal effort and fulfillment is measured between defined lines of hope and time where there never is a feeling of total loss or need to chastise, but rather an effort to understand the differences that roam within this space.

Every day the sun follows its path, crosses over oceans, jungles and desert sands, rides beyond the sounds and chatter of markets in Omdurman and Timbuktu.

Today that burning sunshine covers my garden. On the west side, where it is strongest, and its intensity stays, the papaya trees swell upwards with the thickest of trunks, grow tallest and bear the most fruit. Rich in green and orange and full of yellow, the fruit hangs high encouraging the fig trees and the vegetables below to sap sunshine and bear nature's richness. It is good to have friends that share; it is helpful to be mentored.

I stand near a weather-beaten bamboo trunk—it is upright, old and alone holds a curled hose, a bucket and garden utensils from dangling brackets. I dig a hole for a white metal pole my height to hold a stand on which my solar cooker will rest. A metal post that squirrels and other hungry little creatures cannot climb will rest patiently amongst coral plants and banana trees that hold hands.

It is where they can listen to juices warm, smell homegrown herbs and vegetables cooking and wonder about God's gift of sunshine. This is where I like to cook.

About our globe in distant corners, I shared meals cooked in solar pots, sometimes on the side of roads, in jungle clearings and on the banks of crocodile-infested waters. I ate with strangers, the friendly and the distrustful, till the food satisfied; sometimes till it brought a feeling that softened hesitancy toward new friendship; sometimes till a dancing smile showed past the first brittle words of conversation.

Remarkably in all my travels; at the end of each meal, in different sounding words, voices stretched, guttural or soft, thanks were offered to the spirit of sunshine. In faraway echoes, I still hear the murmurs of those humble people.

In this garden, I have learned to reward myself for personal achievements, to make work creative and divide physical labor into pleasurable intervals. It keeps me interested and enables me to develop an acute awareness of my surroundings, face surprises and hold steady to a discipline timed and adjusted to seasonal changes.

With these changes and the passing of time, I see the way of my garden in its seeds, how compost comforts, why leaves change color, why they fall from branches, leave home. I wonder about my direction.

I see little bits of science wrapped in each leaf, in roots sent deep. I see what is mixed with the sun and the rain that covers my earth and know why seeds, like my fellowmen, can be floaters or sinkers.

Yet, I have unraveled but a thin sweet exciting slice of these mysteries.

My garden table and benches were made from trees that grew in a nearby wood. Sturdy and comfortable, I enjoy them and would not trade them for the world. Sometimes things just come, like those beautiful sounds from the Valley of a Thousand Hills.

These special pieces are from feelings, feelings of a dear neighbor who one day brought wood, tools and labor, but most of all God's gift of creativity.

I followed the craftsman at work and when finished, the last nail hammered, he looked up and said, "This is your gift, my friend."

Like unsolved mysteries, told and retold around the night fires of a thousand tribes, I do not know the origin of feelings.

Today I have learned of their resting place and am forever thankful to the gentle giver. I wear the joy of that visit like a special treasure to share with friends.

The table and benches rest between a cluster of banana and Jatropha trees that look down from their rooftop canopy. Here breezes pass to greet wind gongs and chimes that hang from the thick arms of an oak. For years, their rings and calls have floated between frangipanis and ripening fruit, over squirrel nests and into the den where the opossum sleeps. Their sounds, mixed and melodious, carry tranquility and invite memories.

Sometimes I sit at the table, write, reminisce and think of what has happened and what might have been, knowing that life is like the songs of the gong, no two are the same, each is written with the first sound, and all are as different as every unwritten tomorrow.

Simple thoughts and recollections hold strength and direction. They allow me to recall memories of my garden. I remember how new plants brought butterflies and humming birds. I remember summer shade and places for little critters to hide and nest. I remember the feel of my hoe's wooden handle.

My memories bring a new hope that melts complexity. I am at ease, feel stronger, in control and able to grab the future.

I have learned: some things once cared for, then left alone, develop and return a hundred-fold; garden seeds germinate; the gong writes songs; the solar cooker cooks; and I feel better being self-sufficient, letting things work with the Creator's generosity.

Between writing sentences, I rest and dream. Through time and a distant mist, I see a bridge stretched across a river. It cradles dancing lights, holds soft, the hum of traffic near a tower that climbs toward the stars that once guided me in foreign lands.

Memories come and fade. I sip Pastis, and through its shining drops that drip through sugar, the past clears. Eyes wet, I listen to Edith, "The Little Sparrow," sing "Mon Legionnaire" to me.

Between sips, from this Paris café by the Tour Eiffel, I see what I see, and I listen to the sounds of pounding guns from the desert sands of Africa. I order another.

Some Smiles are for Sadness

The end brings change.

Its shadows move in all directions, some unknown, others planned.

The past is replaced.

New horizons beckon, tempt and call for risk.

Nothing is ever the same.

Through soft shade, sprinkled rays of light dot the ground where women set fresh leaves over damp-smelling soil in the Ituri Forest.

The newborn clings and screams to live a pygmy life, while its mother's head and eyes move to call for assuring arms to wrap its flesh and offer suckling breasts.

A low hum rises, to tell the story of birth and separation from the womb, but soon quietness takes the breeze from the trees. The mother, exhausted, holds pain; and from her heaving body, frailty leaves. Stilled with sudden change, she is gone.

Leaves beneath her hold to the color of trickled blood; the forest stretches upward, erect and motionless. Now there are only murmurs and the sound of weeping women.

On the day I leave my garden, I pray for the arms of the Creator to wrap this space, give each seed and plant sunshine and the opportunity to blossom, to throw perfume.

Like the pygmy spirit that rose with His hand, so too might the next nurturer of this garden be guided to love it, keep its balance, welcome wild bees, fill water barrels and feed ripened fruit to feathered and furry friends.

When I am gone, will someone listen for that murmuring chirp of the lizard family and their call for food? Will hidden seeds be free to lie in secret, waiting for compost? The Martial Eagle, will it ever return?

In the rainy season, will my friendly hopping toad, Gaudeaumus Igitur, come again to share my porch? Will someone comfort him, assure him of his safety, tell him he is free to hop around, free to feed on whatever, and free to go whenever?

Will the bird box attached to the bamboo pole that pulls itself high into the leafy arms of the oak remain the home of Singer the screech owl?

Will someone know, when he does not appear, he is nestled in the palm by the coriander tree?

Settled, he will tell you not to work there. Big pleading eyes will ask, "Why don't you let me sleep?"

I hold tight to the memories and thrills of my garden, know also that on the paths and roads across the plains of Africa, in the currents of its rivers, and in the shadows of its nights, impermanence is written.

Stretched beneath its sky, Providence weaves itself into everything that moves and cries and sings and what might have stood for a million years — and where I see the shadow of this garden.

Today I am new. I embrace humility and awareness. I search for answers and ideas with an intuitive light. I work with opportunities that bud and challenge my talents. I feel steady on this platform of beginning.

Oh! I loved the garden.

I am forever thankful for all we shared and it's giving. Its purpose to redirect me, strengthen weaknesses and accommodate a new start has truly fulfilled itself.

It taught me I was something of value. That I can love. That after change, a new future comes and salty tears of the past dry in the sunshine of time. It taught me desire comes before dreams and intuition is the true guide.

Soon I will leave my garden that sits beside a thin road near a Florida bay. Leaving always tugs and bends a heart with the hurts of loving and departure.

Green and colored, it casts the sweet smell of fresh fruit and the gentle call of herbs that give joy to neighbors and passersby.

If you should come this way, know that its loveliness was not gathered alone, that the Stone of Fabius is buried here.

I go to a little town near a great castle across the ocean to be with new life that blossoms in the most beautiful garden of all. It is the garden of my flesh, of my family, where love grows wild and flows between outstretched arms, where tears fill eyes on smiling faces, share pain and laughter.

Where beauty sits with age; where the newness of our time shades color from beloved past generations and leaves the fine things untouched.

Where the richness of hugs wanders through emotions, where recipes and herbs fill senses, roam the kitchen, and give tastes that linger throughout life.

Where whispered encouragement stays, holds hands with time; where tears come and beg never to forget how we were loved.

I go to a garden from which I can look back, find purity in success, understanding in failure. Where I see hills half climbed, myself on a mountain top, and know, on the river water below where I paddle, there is balance; sometimes reached, sometimes touched, and sometimes only dreamt of.

Here, I find laughter and granddaughters most alluring, most loving, that can soften any heart. It is where I am called Pepe; and now, in this moment, listen to a whisper in my ear.

"Pepe, will you take me to your café? I want to hear to you sing with the legionnaires? Please."

In silence a mother looks up.

"Mama," Calia begins to ask.

"Yes, Calia, you can go, but see Pepe drinks only two Pastis, please."

"Oui, mama."

We sang.

I watched her face blossom, it shone with joy; she clasped my hand then and I felt happier than I had ever been for a long time.

Yes, it visits me often–the far away garden where the frog still sings.